I Wonder Why

Farm Animals

Flip the flaps

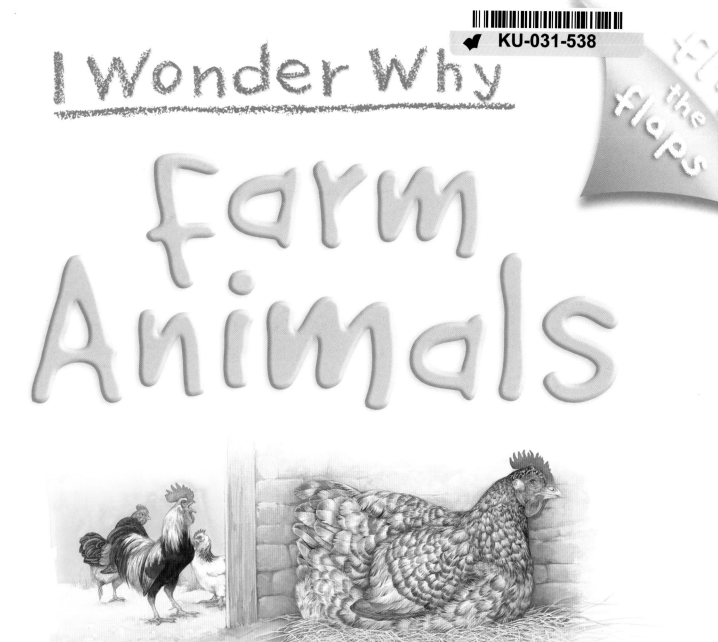

Karen Wallace and Nicki Palin

KINGFISHER

First published 2009 by Kingfisher
an imprint of Macmillan Children's Books
a division of Macmillan Publishers Limited
The Macmillan Building, 4 Crinan Street, London N1 9XW
Basingstoke and Oxford
Associated companies throughout the world
www.panmacmillan.com

Consultant: David Burnie

ISBN 978-0-7534-1685-3

1 3 5 7 9 8 6 4 2
1TR/0908/MPA/UNTD/157MA/C

A CIP catalogue record for this book is available from the British Library.

Printed in China

Contents

Sheep

Many different animals live on a farm. Sheep live outside in the fields all year round, eating grass. Their woolly coats keep them warm. The farmer brings the sheep inside only when they have lambs.

shearing (cutting off) a sheep's coat

sheep in a field

4

1. A fleece is a sheep's woolly coat. It can be made into wool.

2. Some farmers paint spots on their sheep so they can find them if the sheep get lost on another farm.

sheepdog

3. A sheepdog runs around to help the farmer move his sheep.

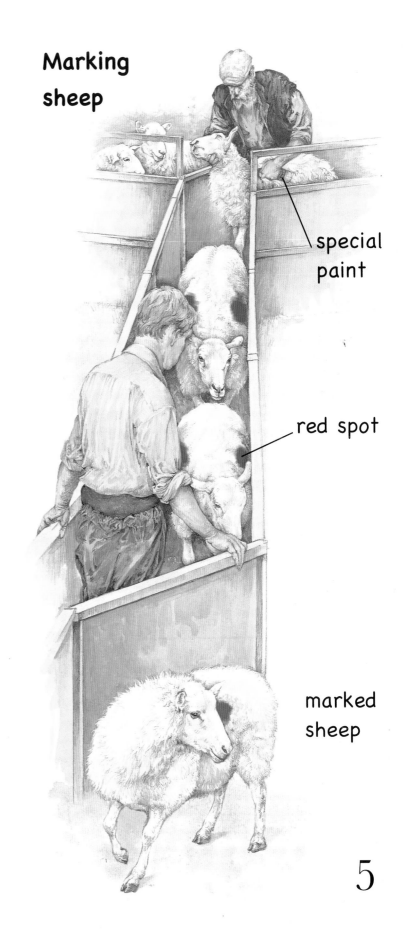

Marking sheep

special paint

red spot

marked sheep

5

Pigs

There are many kinds of pigs. Some pigs are huge and spotty. Others are brown or black-and-white. Most farmers keep large, pink pigs because they have lots of piglets and produce good meat.

pig warming up
in the sunshine

mother pig
sleeping

1. A pig rolls in mud to keep cool and protect its skin from the sun.

2. Pigs eat a mash made of barley and wheat. They also like cabbages and other vegetables.

3. A mother pig has about eight to eleven piglets.

Pigs eating...

mash from a feeder

vegetables from a trough

cabbage from a bucket

Goats

Goats do not like being
alone, so they stay together
in a group, called a herd.
Most farmers keep goats
for their milk, which they
make into cheese.

herd of goats in the mountains

kid
(a baby goat)

horn

beard

two male billy goats

1. Do goats live
   in the mountains
   all year round?

2. What keeps
   goats happy?

3. Why do goats
   have horns?

Goats enjoy...

eating

playing

sleeping

Chickens

At night, chickens sleep
in a special house to keep
them safe from wild animals.
In the morning, the cockerel
wakes them up with a
loud cock-a-doodle-doo!

chicken scratching
the ground

cockerel
(a male chicken)

10

1. Why does a chicken scratch the ground?

...scratches the ...h her feet to find ... worms to eat.

2. What type of feathers do chickens have?

...an have short ...ffy or spotty ...ockerels have ...thers.

3. Why does a mother hen sit on a nest?

...ther hen sits ...r nest to keep ...ggs warm and ...p them hatch.

hen
(a female chicken)

fluffy feathers

spotty feathers

cockerel

long tail feathers

11

Cows

Many farms are home
to a large herd of cows.
In the summer, the cows
live outside in the fields and
eat grass. Baby cows, called
calves, live with the herd.

herd of cows eating grass

eeding a worm
to the chicks

calf drinking its
mother's milk

12

1. What do cows eat in winter?

2. Why do farmers keep cows?

3. How does the farmer get milk from a cow?

Some foods from cows

beef pie

roast beef

beefburger

milk

cheese

yoghurt

butter

Horses

On some farms, horses pull carts or help to plough fields, but on most farms, horses do not work. The farmer and his family enjoy looking after the horses and riding them across the fields.

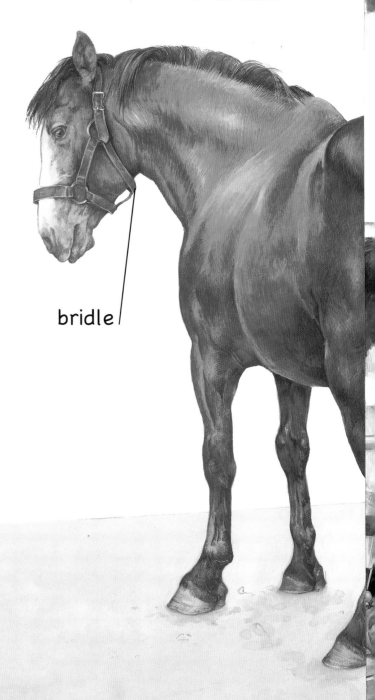

horse wearing a bridle

bridle

tools for looking after the horse's hooves

1. What is a bridle?

s a set of leather
a horse's head.
control the horse.

2. Are there many
kinds of horses?

: are big and
:s, spotty horses,
:ehorses, which
:p very fast.

3. Why does a horse
wear shoes?

A horse wears
metal horseshoes
:o stop its hooves
wearing down.

horseshoe

Some types of horse

shire
horse

Shetland
pony

Appaloosa

racehorse

Ducks

Most farmyard ducks have white feathers and orange beaks. Mallard ducks, which are wild, are different colours. They visit farms to build a nest beside a river or pond.

cleaning feathers with beak

male duck

female duck

mallard ducks swimming in a pond

webbed foot

fitting a horseshoe

1. Why does a duck
clean its feathers?

Ducklings hatching

Ducklings grow inside eggs...

2. When do ducklings hatch?

and then the eggs hatch.

3. Why do ducks have
webbed feet?

The ducklings soon learn to swim.

17

Index